TELL IT SLANT **John Yau**

OMNIDAWN PUBLISHING
OAKLAND, CALIFORNIA
2023

Cover art by Eve Aschheim, "Steel and Soaking" (2013), 18 x 14 inches, oil and graphite on canvas on panel. By permission of the artist.
Cover and interior design by Shanna Compton
Interior typefaces: Adobe Garamond Pro and Museo Sans
Library of Congress Cataloging-in-Publication Data
Names: Yau, John, 1950- author.
Title: Tell it slant / John Yau.
Description: Oakland, California : Omnidawn Publishing, 2023. | Summary: "Emily Dickinson begins one of her best-known poems with the oft-quoted line, "Tell all the truth but tell it slant -" For anyone who is Asian American, the word "slant" can be heard and read two ways. It is this sense of doubleness - culminating in the instability of language and an untrustworthy narrator - that shapes, informs, and inflects the poems, all of which focus on the question of who is speaking and who is being spoken for and to? Made up of eight sections, each of which explores the idea of address - as place, as person, as memory, and as event - Tell It Slant does as Dickinson commands, but with a further twist. Among the summoned spirits who help the author "tell all the truth," the reader will hear reimagined traces of poets, movie stars, and science fiction writers - including Charles Baudelaire, Thomas de Quincey, Philip K. Dick, Li Shangyin, and Elsa Lanchester - among the multitudes contained"-- Provided by publisher.
Identifiers: LCCN 2023019333 | ISBN 9781632431257 (trade paperback)
Subjects: LCGFT: Poetry.
Classification: LCC PS3575.A9 T45 2023 | DDC 811/.54--dc23/eng/20230512
LC record available at https://lccn.loc.gov/2023019333
Published by Omnidawn Publishing, Oakland, California
www.omnidawn.com
10 9 8 7 6 5 4 3 2 1
ISBN: 978-1-63243-125-7

Also by John Yau

POETRY

Sometimes (1979)

Broken Off by the Music (1981)

Corpse and Mirror (1983)

Radiant Silhouette: New & Selected Work 1974–1988 (1989)

Big City Primer (1991), with photographs by Bill Barrette

Edificio Sayonara (1992)

Berlin Diptychon (1995), with photographs by Bill Barrette

Forbidden Entries (1996)

Borrowed Love Poems (2002)

Ing Grish (2005), with Thomas Nozkowski

Paradiso Diaspora (2006)

Further Adventures in Monochrome (2012)

Bijoux in the Dark (2018)

Genghis Chan on Drums (2021)

FICTION

The Sleepless Night of Eugene Delacroix (1980)

Hawaiian Cowboys (1995)

My Symptoms (1996)

My Heart Is That Eternal Rose Tattoo (2001)

CRITICISM

The Passionate Spectator: Essays on Art and Poetry (2006)

The Wild Children of William Blake (2017)

Foreign Sounds or Sounds Foreign (2020)

Please Wait by the Coat Room: Reconsidering Race and Identity in American Art (2023)

COLLABORATIONS

100 More Jokes from the Book of the Dead (2001), with Archie Rand

MONOGRAPHS

In the Realm of Appearances: The Art of Andy Warhol (1993)

A. R. Penck (1993)

Ed Moses: A Retrospective of Paintings and Drawings, 1951–1996 (1996)

The United States of Jasper Johns (1996)

Pat Steir: Dazzling Water, Dazzling Light (2001)

Joan Mitchell: Works on Paper 1956–1992 (2007)

A Thing Among Things: The Art of Jasper Johns (2008)

William Tillyer: Watercolours (2010)

Jay DeFeo: Chiaroscuro (2013)

Mernet Larsen (2013)

Sam Francis (2014)

Richard Artschwager: Into the Desert (2015)

Catherine Murphy (2016)

Al Taylor: Early Paintings (2017)

Thomas Nozkowski (2017)

California Landscapes: Richard Diebenkorn / Wayne Thiebaud (2018)

Philip Taaffe (2018)

William Tillyer: A Retrospective (2021)

Liu Xiaodong (2021)

Joe Brainard: The Art of the Personal (2022)

EDITOR

The Collected Poems of Fairfield Porter (1985), with David Kermani

Fetish (1998)

For my friends born in two worlds

✦

Tell all the truth but tell it slant —

Emily Dickinson

You can't scare me, you slant-eyed yellow bastard.

C.I.A. Agent
The Kentucky Fried Movie (1977)

Contents

I.

Too Far to Write Down

1.

I, humble scribe of clouds, ask permission to make my case

While you scatter ocher cumuli above black orchards and open huts

Pull thick violet brushstrokes through cascading green mountains

I watch my poems ferry fiery farewells downstream

Dream that I am in two places at once, listening

To new ghosts complain there is no room

Until the old ghosts leave their vestments behind

Hear wisps of weeping—wind gathering in mulberry trees

Become wrinkled sheet floating above empty bed

Watch victory and defeat unfurl flags against coal red sky

As moon follows its hollow twin into a waterfall's marbled sections

I turn into drops of ink and snow settling into the repaired space of this poem

2.

I, humble scribe of clouds, ask permission to make my case

It does not matter if the poem's eyes are those of a dead fish

It sees that I am an idle dreamer jilted by flowers stretching far

Sees me patch another layer of gauze to a mulberry tree eaten by moths

Sees me kneel by a river and look at a face waging war with itself, and long ago

I have become a dirty chair on which no one will sit, not even my stuffed parrot

Must I confess that I see you dancing in a poem that I have not yet written

This morning, I began washing away remnants of my cold mountain house

Can this memory become a blue flower floating in a pool of black ink

It is snowing in these poems, which were once branches catching the snow

Unreadable midnight, this part of the world you have not yet bid good-bye

I watch the river changing colors as if it can find inside itself another story to spill

3.

I, humble scribe of clouds, ask permission to make my case

Bamboo forest background, floating arrival, unfurling curlicues

Our ancestors named star clusters after remnants of earlier civilizations

Getting old is no longer a joke even if you have started to become one

I spend all night painting a single blue tear, which I scratch away in the morning

Winter's pewter sky is about to greet us with its roll call of gray

What if a sword can be brighter than the stars—neither will save me

After every rain, snails fill the center of my cottage

Infatuated by your candor, I crawl around my room looking for your shadow

It is like tying a poem to a pigeon's leg and watching it fly in circles

Falling deeper into my foolishness, I begin greeting the brushes and pens

I wake up with an erection and can no longer remember if there was another time

4.

I, humble scribe of clouds, ask permission to make my case

In anticipation of the future, I promise to forget everyone's name

The stars never offer enough clues, which we pick over, furiously, like birds

We want signs of reassurance with tidbits of pleasure strewn throughout

A carcass simmering at the bottom of a pot brought out at the end of every poem

Meanwhile, who will scout the path the painter has left for us to follow

Is the task of the poet to find new ways to turn despair into rice soup

Night settles on the other side of these gnarled mountains

The celestial courtyard where our ancestors sit, awaiting our arrival

Why didn't you write to me when I started bleeding through my paper heart

Who drew this motionless green river outside my window

What absurd errand have you sent me on, now that I have fallen back to earth

5.

I, humble scribe of clouds, ask permission to make my case

The last time I tried to make sense I fell in a ditch and nearly drowned

I did not intend to write a book of insults or draw triangles around "love"

My audience is the vastness and the wine I spill on a table gouged with hearts

I look in the mirror and see a demon behaving as if happiness has no punctuation

My ignorance is older than I am, and it feels stale every time I use it

The point of pointless conversation is to go on as if there is nothing else to attend to

Shall I begin with duck eggs and porcelain spoons now that I am a broken mirror

Pleas, lamentations, and cries—have I become a writer of elegies, a collector of glass tears

There is no need to apply the laws of perspective to these layers of ink and paint

Afraid to look back, a man carries baskets toward a green pool filled with moonlight

He sees rivers and mountains burn into motionless shadows beneath sky's empty shelves

6.

I, humble scribe of clouds, ask permission to make my case

Meteorological changes deliver refuse from another universe

Bird tracks and bamboo scaffolding cast inky red lines on shrinking mountains

Palace rooftop in conversation with cloudy peaks

Moon held in confines of purple robe open at neck

Iridescent glimmer gathered in a tree, waiting for next sign

Sections of jade installed above mother-of-pearl waterfalls

Fine black threads detailing wagon's progress deeper into paint and paper

Moving ladder to another ledge in open courtyard

Days of lengthening shadows and branches ending abruptly

Mountains and bare trees resting on roofs with a boy looking in other direction

Near celestial courtyard where ancestors try to defend rocky paths circling their past

7.

I, humble scribe of clouds, ask permission to make my case

I am a violet silk ribbon holding these sheathes together while coming undone

I am a black lacquer path winding through my aimless disheveled gait

I have started walking to the other side of these mountains with my white writing

I am a wide-eyed boy standing on a bridge glued between two skies

I am a memory becoming a poem becoming a memory lost and forgotten

I am a tile roof washed in swirls of red and gold straw and a puzzled worker

I am maroon and turquoise strands of an unraveling river

I am a bundle of poems left on a straw roof beneath peeling green clouds

I am staring into a bucket of gruel and smiling for no other reason

I am talking to my friend who isn't listening which is why we are friends

I am walking over a stream knowing this page has no other side

i.m. Matthew Wong (1984–2019)

8.

I, humble scribe of clouds, ask permission to make my case

I have stopped listening to my thoughts, which are small and unfriendly

I followed you until I realized it was not you I was following

I don't love the blossoms enough that I want to catch them when they fall

In the distance a house sits beneath an approaching meteor of paint

I have not bathed in months and still I don't smell like I am alive

I don't need to try and remember the taste of dirt

A ragged string of birds is erasing itself in the folded mist

I am tempted to make sense, however brief and foolish that might seem

I climb a mountain bending beside a river and never leave my table

I set this poem beneath ink-patterned sky made of paper and stone

Whatever I have written on will be torn apart and covered over

II. *Forms of Address*

Song for Mie Yim

This morning they released my head
from the closet where the university
stores last century's computers
lesson books proven wrong

I am told I have become a gas station
in a city powered by electric cars
an overdue library card

You are born
        shoulders
            tears
                clocks

You learn different ways
you are unnecessary

You don't need
to memorize them

I have been told my head
is being moved
to a better location
being introduced into
warm, welcoming environs

I can sing
as much

as I want
I have been told
this is what
it was like for poets
in an earlier time

Now it is different
I am told
Now it is better

Meadow Gathering

These are nothing more
than dandelions of distraction
insinuated into the wind

Listen, malicious matadors
professors of droopy eyelids
unwieldy viewers possessed by final images

does anyone remember why
a martyr of little accomplishment
became the cornerstone of the poet's conception of grief?

why people still roar
at the sound of
an idol's name?

Or is there
some other reason
why we are here?

Come, stick your oar in the green and yellow
mud of today's lies and disasters
Explain yourself, beginning at the bottom.

Charles Baudelaire and I Meet in the Oval Garden

Which windowpane are you beating your wings against today?
I am not as stubborn as you: I am flying straight into that delicious fire.

Buckets of bubbling tar and champagne await us at the *Blue Chalet*.
Do you skip like this because you have been invited into our lovely little choir?

I am not as stubborn as you: I am flying straight into that delicious fire.
I thought you were going to the theater in your new cabriolet.

Do you skip like this because you have been invited into our lovely little choir?
Yes, I do know the difference between a martini and a matinee.

I thought you were going to the theater in your new cabriolet.
They say that the latest strain hiding in the shadows is a yellow vampire.

Yes, I do know the difference between a martini and a matinee.
You have your subdivisions and high rises, while I have my shire.

They say that the latest strain hiding in the shadows is a yellow vampire.
Don't worry— my ancestors are sewn up in overcoats and on full display.

You have your subdivisions and high rises, while I have my shire.
When it comes to curry and gin, I say: "Let's wallow in Combray."

Don't worry—my ancestors are sewn up in overcoats and on full display.
Which windowpane are you beating your wings against today?

When it comes to curry and gin, I say: "Let's wallow in Combray"
Buckets of bubbling tar and champagne await us at the *Blue Chalet*

After Thomas De Quincey

Discourteous reader and moral ulcer, spurious human frailty
Spoon-fed sponge cake drawn from pustulating postulant
Gratuitous self-humiliation written in every form of failed masturbation
Hands grown icy to clutch in infectious language of penitential loneliness
Do I claim too large a fellowship for the short days I am here
My head snapped shut, no longer in honorable preserve
Open to every driveling reproach, being a member of the slant
So blended and twisted are these occasions of laughter and tears
Recurring dream of walking beside yourself, party to forcible
Departures, your body's suitcase cramped, old sock, splintered dung
Not a dream within a dream of possible slender regimen
This coffee impregnated morning, under sign of unspared trouble
Now that trepidation is latest old friend to suck on your infirmities
Within few hastily assembled steps gratified to expose
Latest spectacle of gratuitous scars, soapy scads of guilt
Misery given public notice, while clocking its fascinating effects
On pastel gossip dens, sounds of interference redoubled
Strewn with pills, pink polka dots of appeasement, at thirteen
I too spoke with ease to no avail, a bellowing blockhead
Glued in ancient panic, ransacking the compass diction
Extracting treatises underlined with decaying manners
Discovering what I wish would arrive cordially impaired
Constant revelry has no need of good breeding, remote from
Prize money announcements of confidential winners
No strings, no attachment, no lovely cottage blushes
Or farsighted hospitalities, seems disposed to dwindle
On second reading, shall I repeat my advice, its accursed letters
Stamped again and again with pride and astonishment

Philip K. Dick's Last Earthly Appearance

for Andrew Joron

I am reprocessing my life, after being glued inside a copy of Dante's *Inferno*
Another writer sentenced to rewrite his novels as sick cheapo hack

In order to buy a house, drive a Buick Jetmaster, and wear a suit and tie
How can I prove that he and I dream the same colors and kiss the same crooked air?

Another writer sentenced to rewrite his novels as sick cheapo hack
An orderly congress of money piles, neat towers illuminating a convoluted situation

How can I prove that he and I dream the same colors and kiss the same crooked air?
I confess to containing at least one other truly unsavory human being

An orderly congress of money piles, neat towers illuminating a convoluted situation
It doesn't help that I can recall instances dating back 2000 years or more

I confess to containing at least one other truly unsavory human being
What if his world is my heaven and my world is his heaven?

It doesn't help that I can recall instances dating back 2000 years or more
I sometimes crash into cobblestone streets and hansom cabs when this happens

What if his world is my heaven and my world is his heaven?
I will start by traveling to earth to prove my visions are entirely real

I sometimes crash into cobblestone streets and hansom cabs when this happens.
I am reprocessing my life, after being glued inside a copy of Dante's *Inferno*

I will start by traveling to earth to prove my visions are entirely real
In order to buy a house, drive a Buick Jetmaster, and wear a suit and tie

Memories of Charles Street, Boston

One day I wake up and my hair has turned white
and I am no longer Chinese

I want to ask my mother about this change in my appearance
but she has been dead longer than I have been alive

You have to take the good with the bad she used to tell me
before trying to drown me in the bathtub

My father sat in the next room in his imported black underwear
smoking a perfumed cigar

and jerking off in front of the television
he had dragged in from the street

It never worked. It still doesn't, and the blue stains on the chair
are why I never sit there

The Sweetness of Unheard Music

As a child, I was told that
if I sang for my supper

I would be fed what the others
at the table were eating

Big plates and large ladles
would be mine to use

I did not need to
wash my hands

Later, as an adult,
I was told that

because my voice
would stir up mayhem

bedlam was where
I would end up

I acted as if I believed
what I heard

from the authorities
who had never heard me sing

nor pretended to
my secret happiness

After I Turned 71
for Laura Mullen

I did not expect to see myself standing before a mirror

I look like someone I would never want to meet

I wonder if I have made a mistake without knowing it

I am sure the word "disaster" does not tell the whole story

I know there is room for improvement but I decide to skip over that part

I realize this passport is the last one that will be issued to me

I begin to think the joke is not only on me

I can walk in any direction and still end up in the wrong place

I stop trying to make a list of words I will never use again

I decide making sense is no longer an acceptable form of lying

I think it is prudent to let others do the counting

I often tell strangers that I might start vomiting when the seasons begin to change

I agree that "reincarnation" is a scam perpetuated by life insurance companies

I liked it when the cab driver called me "young man" and gave him a smaller tip

A Song I Heard Myself Singing

Come, rest your drowned head in my basket
I will bring it down to the tavern tonight
Wrapped in a blue and gold silk scarf

I will tend the tears you never cried
I will wave off the mites looking for
blood still bubbling in your veins

Come, rest your drowned head in my basket
I will shed the tears you never cried
But I won't sing your praises

No, I won't sing your praises
Nor will I pray for a better future
Come, rest your drowned head in my basket

Years Later

I did not know
you were gone

The voice said
There is no one here now

please don't leave
another message

Confessional Poem

It's true. I belong to the last tribe of Chinamen known as "The Inscrutables"
If you are reading this message, you know there is no answer to the question

Why not! Our relationship is parasitical. You have the stingers and I have the lotions
Do you want to continue being part of this conversation or don't you

If you are reading this message, you know there is no answer to the question
If you do not reply immediately, I will take a hint and get lost in a traffic jam

Do you want to continue being part of this conversation or not?
I prefer to lie face down in the mud when a tropical rainstorm stops to visit

If you do not reply immediately, I will take a hint and get lost in a traffic jam
Do you realize that eating bananas in public is a cliché gesture that needs editing?

I prefer to lie face down in the mud when a tropical rainstorm stops to visit
The last time I had a strong sense of vocation was when I went on an unpaid vacation

Do you realize that eating bananas in public is a cliché gesture that needs editing?
I have never quite felt free of my own nature, even when I cannot grasp it

The last time I had a strong sense of vocation was when I went on an unpaid vacation
Will I ever learn to satisfy the bad taste you display on every occasion

I have never quite felt free of my own nature, even when I cannot grasp it
It's true. I belong to the last tribe of Chinamen known as "The Inscrutables"

Will I ever learn to satisfy the bad taste you display on every occasion
Why not! Our relationship is parasitical. You have the stingers and I have the lotions

Chinatown Blues

Don't keep saying poetry makes nothing happen
I am not trying to be your surrogate chaplain

I am going to grow up and be a hatchet man
Doing the sharp and shiny thing—being the best I can

Don't tell me the wood is far too green or yellow
Or that Mr. Frost—protector of fences—is a jolly good fellow

I am still going to grow up and tell it slant
Don't even try and tell me I can't

Stop reminding me I have to watch what I say
Be polite or I will have to pay and pay

I am still going to grow and be a hatchet man
Doing the sharp and shiny thing—being the very best I can

III.

A Painter's Thoughts (6)
(after Peter Saul)

I was searching my brain for some unexpected subject matter
I'm 86 and in grave danger of appearing elderly and demented

Unless you can come up with some subject you haven't done, even as a child
Flowers, for example, I haven't looked at them, much less painted them

I am 86 and in grave danger of appearing elderly and demented.
I am avoiding the reality that in a mere 14 years I'll be dead

Flowers, for example, I haven't looked at them, much less painted them
I got right to work, the usual careless distortions, on purpose or not

I am avoiding the reality that in a mere 14 years I'll be dead
It turns out that flowers are just as good subjects as flying saucers

I got right to work, the usual careless distortions, on purpose or not
It doesn't matter that nobody's fooled, because I am at least artistically

It turns out that flowers are just as good subjects as flying saucers
Right now, I'm thinking of God and Superman battling it out above an American city

It doesn't matter that nobody's fooled, because I am at least artistically
Who wants to think about how much will be destroyed at a time like this

Right now, I'm thinking of God and Superman battling it out above an American city
I was searching my brain for some unexpected subject matter

Who wants to think about how much will be destroyed at a time like this
Unless you can come up with some subject you haven't done, even as a child

A Painter's Thoughts (7)
(after Lois Dodd)

It is someone else's subject if you think it would look good if they painted it
If I work on this painting longer, it would be perfect and no longer mine

I am with my thin paint. Putting on a second coat will shut out the light
Morandi's paintings are wonderful, but they have not influenced me

If I work on this painting longer, it would be perfect and no longer mine
I admire juicy paint on other people's canvases, but that's not what I do

Morandi's paintings are wonderful, but they have not influenced me
Even if I never tell a story, my feelings and emotions will come through

I admire juicy paint on other people's canvases, but that's not what I do
In the beginning it was cows, just cows. Now it's human beings

Even if I don't tell a story, my feelings and emotions will come through
I don't want fancy stuff, or even a lot of stuff. Don't blame the abstract artists for this

In the beginning it was cows, just cows. Now it's human beings
I don't like distant views; I wouldn't be happy going to the top of a mountain

I don't want fancy stuff, or even a lot of stuff. Don't blame the abstract artists for this
The easel was there, I thought, well, this is fun: here I am painting myself painting.

I don't like distant views; I wouldn't be happy going to the top of a mountain
It is someone else's subject if you think it would look good if they painted it

The easel was there, I thought, well, this is fun: here I am painting myself painting
I am with my thin paint. Putting on a second coat will shut out the light

A Painter's Thoughts (8)
(after Sylvia Plimack Mangold)

I work hard to keep the pictorial element out of my work
How to paint leaves has been a dilemma since I started painting trees

If I finish it next summer, I will have to repaint the whole painting
I have to, because the tree is growing, the light is changing

How to paint leaves has been a dilemma since I started painting trees
The form of the trunks and branches is so sculptural

I have to, because the tree is growing, the light is changing
Nature can be very romantic; it's hard to get away from it

The form of the trunks and branches is so sculptural
I would get so I'd be looking forward to winter

Nature can be very romantic; it's hard to get away from it
It's exciting the way that paint flies across the surface and just lands

I would get so I'd be looking forward to winter
And then I just sort of faced up to painting every leaf

It's exciting the way that paint flies across the surface and just lands
I traded my trading card collection for a set of oil paints

And then I just sort of faced up to painting every leaf
I work hard to keep the pictorial element out of my work

I traded my trading card collection for a set of oil paints
If I finish it next summer, I will have to repaint the whole painting

A Painter's Thoughts (9)
(after Robert Mangold)

I've never been involved in paint the way a lot of painters are
Drawing is the starting point. Paint is a step, a way of coloring a surface

I'm never sure how I got into doing the circle paintings
It may have come from that summer where I was just looking at nature

Drawing is the starting point. Paint is a step, a way of coloring a surface
It's always a dual thing, a kind of container and then an image in the container

It may have come from that summer where I was just looking at nature
I thought of brick color, the color of cardboard, or of a manila envelope

It's always a dual thing, a kind of container and then an image in the container
There was a sense that everything suddenly became subject matter

I thought of brick color, the color of cardboard, or of a manila envelope
I wondered, should my color be coming from file cabinets

There was a sense of that everything is suddenly became subject matter
Along with the shape there is the idea of what's going to go in it

I wondered, should my color be coming from file cabinets
I've never been involved in paint the way a lot of painters are

Along with the shape there is the idea of what's going to go in it
I'm never sure how I got into doing the circle paintings

IV.

Li Shangyin Enters Manhattan

1.

I am a parakeet in a cave, malaise's candle flame,
An open letter to myself who is you: poets always
Need to be foreign, even in their own country
I was walking into a candy store when I bumped into
Another dance of ink I will never join in fragrant ceremony
Drips of soot filling clouds of yesterday's imagination
Can you sing "of" in a downloaded song and not sound
Like you are a native speaker lost in an alley
With two entrances, one of which is your mouth
I comb streets of sand and pollen, looking for flowers
Whose petals possess a remedy for dreams
Filled with poorly transcribed instructions guaranteed
To make every devourer wish life could be written in reverse
Do you know whose glossolalia you will be speaking in today

2.

The greatest poet in Chinese history
Is a mulberry tree on which poems
Are sprinkled in ash, ink, or snow
Walking to corner movie palace
Talking to ladybugs, humming rhymes
To radio operators, whistling standards
For plankton mechanics under pine sap sky
I stop and watch a clowder of polluted cats
Swimming upstream, in search of better furniture
I squat in a cold bath and imagine I am a poet
A talking tree writing sonnets for humankind
An atomic clock sitting on a rock in paradise
Announcing, this is the blue mirror in which
You will see yourself spinning all your fault lines

3.

Why do you say this scroll of painted mulberry bark
Is a trembling lake deaf to ink splashes and falling sun
Have you ever talked to coroners of silkworms
Children who only watch movies in rearview mirrors
Gardeners who tend to weeds growing through gravestones,
Waiters who refuse to serve real or substitute meat
What side of your face aches from obedience issues
What milestone did you reach when your heart
Turned to ash, and you wrote: "even the fog is blight"
Are poets still underpaid to operate levers of
A dead language machine, kill doves when
They think the festooned little plumps are laughing
More silver lacerations refilling night's placard bowl
Memory's janitors sweeping away sights of wounds and ruins

4.

I like extended confinement, days of walking around
In clown polka dots and clean underwear, as thinking
Arrives in nibbled sheathes, occult graphite, amber
Globules of ancient sweat, swiped blocks of innuendo
I stood on one leg, like a drain pipe, cranking candor
Into steam, always out of kilter in hubbub and morass
But not here, in my amulet chamber, when heaven
Is no longer a glass ceiling to throw yellow lumps against
Watch beige moon's limping stone in gravel sky
Escape to goblin screen whistling with digital sparks
Tomes piled in parking lot, where your customized chassis
Fled rising palaver, what say you now slant-eyed cow
Or goads to that effect still played out on media grab
Serving mixed grill's nightly tapestry of feral apologies

5.

More huts of blather retreat into latest urban sob story
Night arrives full of carbon stains in leaking tank
What winged shadow brushed against your diesel chariot
What upright little god of the hearth did you swear at today
Who requested extra sets of hands to squeeze birds
Squawking right out of life, their carbonated spit splintering the air,
Midnight hearse hauling their little crystal coffins back to
Seaweed banks, where you and your throttle of soulful bleeders
Have to sing for your package, no magnetic stripes please
That is the repeat glutton pressing the unheated lips of
Your baffled pocket mouth, your cold distress
Burn down legions of last overcoats, their headless shoes
There is nothing thicker than sickness dripping against
The blackened bulkhead of this gutted rickshaw

6.

I keep my remaining glands in a jar by the nightstand
I live in a condo villa and drink tall glasses of cold plum juice
Give me edible sermons and I will recycle your sentiments
Display another filament binge as I grind the heart loose
Pick slips of masticated plastic from plates of steaming viscera
These are slippery hills we are hooked forward to
Lumps and bones spilling lard of our common stock market
Lined with barnacles and crackling bunkum, courtesy of old world ways,
My name is Captain Manatee, Oboe Steam House, Elgin Relic,
I sing and fly in the opera known as the Lost United Fates
Picketed gates or heads on plates, weigh down upon
Stack of whitened swans, headline pileup with more bash-ins
Suspects speak of terminal clutter, but comic relief is when
You don't pee in your pants by a flooded highway

7.

I inherited yellow shack and shabby body no one wanted to move into
I took up residence there, as cubits of greased windpipes sounded
Their pavement splatter, and I decided on glow-in-the-dark pencils
As fast track to masterpiece and high-yield cash return
While ogling owls earmarked by smoke rinsed skyline
I have got a carpet I can wear to the good riddance store
O producer of precious toil, did you drink your barium today
I don't keep socks in a drawer and I don't keep stocks in a portfolio
I don't believe earth is a barbell you hoist to heaven's penthouse suite
Birth is when you receive your first distortion, how many days
In a peep show did you keep your glistening bristles behind sludge pump
Post and bean bracket tractor fish fill the dreaming pond
Don't fall asleep beside your latest broken paragraph,
You never know when a stone might fall out of the blinking sky

8.

What makes you think jumping bean shortages
Causes severe head swivel, why inflame porridge
Brain to cry over its swelling drive, when I am left
Asking where does someone stand on subway platform
When nowhere Is safe, past and future long absconded
And the summer of us that do not feel quite at home
Eating in refrigerated diners, scouting horizontal closets,
Photographing massage pyramids stamped with free pizza delivery
Is this what you call a big tent, three-in-one garbage camp
Another promised deposit in bank of staved and craven
Thick as thought balloon's empty gloat
Do I have to respect the whites of your lies
Forget that I forgot about difference between fiction and flying
In shadow lips still spawning on hate night TV

9.

Greetings, goodbye kitty, your little paw gloved in golden armor,
Will you welcome latest dwelling in animal squalor
It is one thing to be a fly on an elephant, O furless dust ball,
But when you are an elephant on the fly, can you still cram
Dust back into fire's high yield maw, repeat spin
Cycle of eating and spitting out humans trying to
Imitate life without achieving mechanical efficiency
Do you hear footsteps following you into foyer of waiting dream
See a beetle standing on its hind legs, waving its barbed wires
When future generations pry apart this desert with their wands
Will they find rancid city spilled into eight-sided gas stations
Histories of chained reactions, motor pools of cadaverous rain
Obit slobber, when did you become today's white elephant
Preparing to be an icicle banging against infinity's garage door

10.

I wrote a memoir and got up without incident
I stood on a balcony and watched a cow dump over the moon
I smoked a wet cigar and climbed into a shiny red jalopy
I waved goodbye and ran madly into the wilds of a poem
I checked birth certificates and stacked pancakes
The size of my thumb. When nothing happened
In the cauldron I was stirring, a piece of clumsy fog,
I climbed into next room, and sang to the cactus
I pretended to be an ecstatic semaphore waving
On front door of used stamp and calendar shop
Shelves full of last year's weather vanes, expired
Smoke detectors, split bundles of medicinal poisons
I learned to become someone else I was never
Meant to be: I began wallowing in your shoes

11.

Spray can subway sign: Living is wheezing
A horse riding through swollen veins
I press on and leave gold hand prints
Against sky's black pocket, write poems
On brick piles, I am not like the others
Who drift from horny to scorn in a blink
Another slammed drunk upended
In romance's spreading muddle
The life of a Chinese cowboy
Isn't all chopped duck and pinto schemes,
I have seen many boys, dead and alive
Crying a thousand deaths, stripped blue in the rain
But I still love the smoky smell of a fireman's rubber coat
Crispy french fries lathered in mustard and mayonnaise

i.m. Martin Wong (1946–1999)

12.

I watch cities and towns billboarding their future
As if every dream of a golden past can catch up
And settle in, deal another round of further ado
On the gravy boat parade stitched conglomeration
These globs are aimed at your heirloom bowl
Why be curious when furious is easier on your face
When did you learn your aspirations are onerous
Residue of swarming crowds, salted visitations,
Assaulted cannisters of human ash, brained aprons,
Lessons In lesions, amassed constellations
Cold swarms of thought left over from
Previous chronicles, having outlived sunlight's
Latest crime, this is America stalling, do you
Still have room for an inflated penis to hitch a ride

13.

Botched courts erase rows of empty bellybuttons
Was it you garbed in latest sweatshop imports
Blinking at dangled specimens of five-star gene selection
Loosening your prose to gauge upscale climbing in firearm rehab,
Bliss stalks its custom loafers in ever-widening
Rings of borrowed sentiment, real estate is the real state
No matter how you fluff its entrails,
Don't hurry if your name is mud and you caught a cold
In the late afternoon, as I prefer sitting inside stone cottage
Or basking beside a pond when sun slips into a fire truck
To finish masturbating, that's when I unscrew my skull
Place it on table, turn off my beady yellow eyes, fall
Into myself, do you ever feel that your life is not worth
Stealing back, not the slightest reflection left behind

14.

I left the drugstore and went and sat in the park
What language of waste had I been listening to,
Without hearing what is there, day's grinding crust
Depositing scales of human skin on sills and in our hair
Constant swirl we sit and stand in, move through
Our ancestors all around us, waiting to be swept up
Once again, from sidewalk and chair, barbershop
Pile up of hair, dust on hair, and in the air around us
What we lose of our bodies does not come back
Leave something behind each moment you breathe,
Even in sleep shedding continues, even in this poem,
Which I wrote before we met and after we parted
What happened in that interval I still circle around
Blossoms of magenta dust lifted to your lips

V. Language Lessons

After Wang Wei

I am not exactly sure when I left the clouds behind
I must have fallen for a long time and had many dreams
But I do not remember slow dripping clocks
Or small formations of silent egrets winging their way
To the land of a thousand estuaries brimming with tears

I had to learn these things by looking at paintings and reading poems
I had to close my door, draw the curtains, and sit in the dark
I had to climb towers and pore over remnants
Deposited by a burning sky, while the mountains
Grew darker and the seas began to boil

When I got old, I began thinking about the clouds I left behind
To see what traces of my passing I might discover
I decided to quit my post and leave my desk to the leaves
Today, walking past potholes and barricades,
I dream once again of seesaws and autumn rain

Sun Worshippers

They are our representatives to the life-giving sun
That blazing biscuit baking for our benefit
They are priests and priestesses reveling in our name.
We use social media to select the ones we want to follow
Vicarious participants in their sybaritic rituals of frolic and relax
We watch them enter turquoise waters from a fringe of fine white sand
Their baptism of delight is the prayer they send to the sun on our behalf
Our thwarted desire to be bathed in its motherly light and fatherly warmth
We watch them, like rescue dogs given a new life: this is our worship
We want to be like them; this is our fervent longing for transcendence
To be delivered to the land of everlasting light
To no longer be tailless and panting in the dark
Looking down a long unlit hall
While sitting beside the pantry
Furiously scratching our ears and licking our paws
As if we were infested with self-inflictions
They send us pictures so that we know where they are and what they are doing
They embrace our love and accept that they cannot be out of our sight
They let us follow them around and see what they are shopping for
They send us signals, emblems and insignias
They teach us what to spend our money on
How to follow in their footsteps
from a worshipful distance
And for this we are thankful

Third Language Lesson

The difference between being bought and being a bot is a glass of spilled milk
You must try and step away from the puddle in which you will one day drown

From Zoom to Zombie—someone on our staff can help you find what you need
Please sit by the window, count midges or carve numbers out of rice

You must try and step away from the puddle in which you will one day drown
Don't forget your shadows at twilight: you can begin with your seedless stump

Please sit by the window, count midges or carve numbers out of rice
The Spartans invented the concept of destination in order to imitate ants

Don't forget your shadows at twilight: you can begin with your seedless stump
You don't have to know what day it is unless you have a doctor's appointment

The Spartans invented the concept of destination in order to imitate ants
When did you start storing expired cans of insect repellent under the sink

You don't have to know what day it is unless you have a doctor's appointment
I told you that I am listening to money and birds falling from the sky

When did you start storing expired cans of insect repellent under the sink
When did I begin looking for myself beneath the kitchen table

I told you that I am listening to money and birds falling from the sky
I have eaten cheap bread many times but this is the first time I have tasted it

When did I begin looking for myself beneath the kitchen table
After the road turned into the sky, it started raining and diluted everyone's cheers

I have eaten cheap bread many times but this is the first time I have tasted it
To begin in diapers and to end in diapers doesn't mean you had a good life

After the road turned into the sky, it started raining and diluted everyone's cheers
The difference between being bought and being a bot is a glass of spilled milk

To begin in diapers and to end in diapers doesn't mean you had a good life
From Zoom to Zombie—someone on our staff can help you find what you need

Dream Report

1.

I never told you about the time I met you in a dream. We were nearing Shanghai. At least that is what the red signs said, the ones we could read, which popped up every now and then, after miles of passing large green-and-white combinations we did not understand, even if they predicted the hour and day of our demise. You said you were not expecting to see me on this train, but on the one coming back. How did you know that I was going to be in Shanghai? I asked. It is not a subject we have ever discussed in all our years of doing business. We didn't have to, you said. It is written all over your face. You have never been able to wash those tears away, no matter how many times you have tried.

2.

I do not remember many of my dreams, hardly any, in fact, less than a handful, most likely because they don't want to be trapped here, in a world pierced by sunlight.

3.

I keep thinking that I should meet a living poet in this alternative world, perhaps my good friend who lives in Singapore or the one whose books I have been reading from cover to cover (there are more of these than you might think), but I keep encountering poets who have died, some who left just a few days or weeks ago, no matter where I am transported: Hollywood movie set or abandoned beehive redesigned as a library, rubble strewn parking lot in Ecuador or leafy forest trail in Wales, places that know me well. These poets feel that they did not get enough attention during their lifetime, and they have decided to lurk around in dreams, hoping to alter the future of their afterlife in the world they left behind.

4.

I met my grandfather, who excelled at water maintenance, only once, long after he had died alone in the old city of Hong Kong, after years of wandering to starlit domains: Bristol, where he was the first Chinese to graduate the university; New York, where he became a father; Hoboken, where he walked underground and looked at gauges and pipes; Beijing, where he lost his smile; and Shanghai, where he lost his family. I asked him if he had any advice on how I should live my life. He smiled wanly, looked at his feet, and shook his head. No, I have no advice. He broke his smile with another, traces of bitterness visible in his hesitations. I myself have failed at everything I ever did, he said in a soft voice: studying, marriage, civil engineering, being a father to my only child, who left before I could say goodbye. In fact, I even flopped rather badly as a grandfather, which is why we have not met until now.

5.

Did you get the poem I sent you, you asked, incredulous that I had not read it and could not make any comment—intelligent or otherwise—on its structural beauty? Really, you sneered sarcastically. Poets are all alike, you hissed through gritted teeth, but decided no further explanation was necessary.

The Multicolored Rays of Postindustrial Life

In the opening scene, a calico cat climbs onto a window ledge and looks down at the situation below, a briefcase begins unfolding the eight corners of its stolen hexagon, trying to glimpse its future. On the imported Chinese-made television glowing uneasily in the other room, an unshaven man (or is it a recently dead actor?) pulls a knife out of his neatly pressed trousers and smiles in the mirror, where, behind him, a Cold War UFO can be glimpsed hovering above a circular police station designed by an imitator of Frank Lloyd Wright who pursued the goodness found in civic outbursts. A refrigerator's ice machine drops its latest payload. Two blocks to the east, if such a direction still exists in this accelerating time frame, three dogs of various sizes and breeds begin barking, angry because the drug dealers are trying to make a living near their beloved mailbox, favored site of their last nightly expulsion until the sun peers over the horizon, a red-faced drunk splattering the air with unwanted news. Words are exchanged, but no money. You liked it better when the kangaroos dressed in blue leather jackets and matching shorts, wore epaulets and peaked caps. It was reassuring to hear them in the hours before dawn, hopping about in tight formation, the rhythmic thumping calming the nerves of the nomadic worshipful praying for *The End* to appear in perfect script in the silver sky above, plugging into the armadas of hammers waiting to be released into the hands of the righteous. This was the B movie you had been waiting for as summer slid into the fall, the sun moving further and further away. You had watched the trailer repeatedly, thinking its extended teaser might add another scene as the calendar deposited its predictable contents into the mouths of unsuspecting infants, and they spewed forth their announcements. You began scripting your own scenes full of plot twists and sweaty encounters, because this is what individuals in your age group did at night. It was a romance you had rehearsed countless times, even as you acted oblivious to the interruptions rolling past you on the days your nerves crackled and your skin flared. Each morning your dreams got up and fled before you could catch sight of them. You lay in your bed wondering if there were other ways time could be made to trickle through your fingers. One evening, you woke up on the floor beside your bed, wondering how you got there, your legs embraced by waves of dervish fur. An uninvited guest who knows what you have been dreaming about is greeting you with an extraordinarily beautiful set of teeth. All along the audience has seen what you have been writing down on small pages, in the rising red dark. Now each of them steps forward, as in a play about small town life, and eagerly tells you about a cat perched on a windowsill, what it sees on the street far below, and how you have come to be where you are, in clothes borrowed from a lover (not yours) whose name is tattooed on your back, where you can read it backwards in a mirror, and perhaps absorb one more lesson about the laws of dynamic distribution.

Public Restroom Blues

I don't mean to be personal about this but don't you think you have been inside that bathroom long enough to cause the centipede forming out here to have accumulated a beachfront of second thoughts, beginning with—the next-in-line neighbor's rising crescendo—a small matter regarding the taxonomy of animals decomposing in an adjacent yard, where no one can see their matted demeanor, but which have led to a pride of staunchly cadaverous neighbors ("don't you mean conservative?") to petition the mayor about passing an ordinance forbidding certain smells to have any influence over one's hard-earned lifestyle, a law that would extend to butchers and abattoirs, when called for.

Listen, I do not belong to the club that prefers the breasts and buttocks seen in paintings be varnished with a liquid that protects them from aging. Some of us grow old and some of us die before becoming a postscript. The children are laughing because they have run out of other responses to the smell of compost. Once you weren't a dunce, but that was long ago, in another life that was the beginning of your eternal dissatisfaction, which does not explain why you cling to your obstinance with Cossack fervor. Are you trying to get me to relax by bringing up all these thorns sticking out of your paw? Remember to look back, before leaving. The entire personality of a mirror lies with the amputation standing before it.

View from the Balcony

We don't know how often civilizations kill themselves, just that they do
We seldom stop and calculate moon's cold light traveling across the night sky

Thomas Edison is to blame: electric lights turned our attention away from the stars
Counting them is tedious. How many do you think are lurking in clouds and dust?

We seldom stop and calculate moon's cold light traveling across the night sky
Certain types of stars are like old cars, leaking carbon molecules into interstellar space

Counting them is tedious. How many do you think are lurking in clouds and dust?
There are more elephants in this room than the vastness can theoretically hold

Certain types of stars are like old cars, leaking carbon molecules into interstellar space
Ferdinand Magellan reported seeing bright circular clusters in the Southern Hemisphere

There are more elephants in this room than the vastness can theoretically hold
Most other civilizations that still exist in the galaxy today are likely young

Ferdinand Magellan reported seeing bright circular clusters in the Southern Hemisphere
Movie stars in films swap spit, but who knew that galaxies swap stars

Most other civilizations that still exist in the galaxy today are likely young
The origin of our galaxy is so old we do not what roads it took to get here

Movie stars in films swap spit, but who knew that galaxies swap stars
We're likely a frontier civilization in terms of galactic geography

The origin of our galaxy is so old we do not what roads it took to get here
We are relative latecomers to the self-aware Milky Way inhabitant scene

We're likely a frontier civilization in terms of galactic geography
We don't know how often civilizations kill themselves, just that they do

We are relative latecomers to the self-aware Milky Way inhabitant scene
Thomas Edison is to blame: electric lights turned our attention away from the stars

VI.

Elsa and Charles with Cameo by Tallulah

My favorite moment in *The Bride of Frankenstein* (1935), directed by James Whale, and starring Boris Karloff (naturally) as the Monster and frizzy-haired Elsa Lanchester (who also plays the author Mary Shelley at the start of the film) as his betrothed, is when the young bride looks up at her towering, misunderstood hubby and vehemently whispers: "I hate you, you oversized piece of imitation luggage." The monster begins crying at the sight of the young woman gyrating wildly before him, pounding his massive chest with her tiny fists, before reaching over and pulling a shiny black switch, which sends waves of sparking voltage shooting throughout the laboratory and Gothic tower where they are standing, turning it into a camera close-up of granite blocks, burning desks and papers, broken beakers, bottles of potions and powders, and what might be the mingling of the monster and his angry bride's limbs.

It does not matter that this did not happen in the film because it is very easy to imagine Lanchester doing something outrageous and memorable, as it was an epidemic running through her family. She was the daughter of James Sullivan and Edith Lanchester, socialists who refused to legalize their union in stuffy, rule-bound England, although they happily stayed together until one preceded the other in death without thinking that heaven awaited them. When Edith's family learned of her plans to live with James without being married in a church or standing before a magistrate (she was by then a confirmed atheist who believed "marriage" would deprive her of her freedom), they kidnapped her and had her certified as insane at the Priory Hospital in Roehampton. The cause of her "insanity" was listed as "over-education." This did not deter Edith in the least, and the case caused a national scandal. According to the *New York Times*, Edith's incarceration "rivet[ed] the attention of three kingdoms" that "no penny paper had printed less than ten columns on this engrossing subject during the week" Edith was incarcerated and abused. After Edith was released, she got a job as the private secretary of Eleanor Marx, Karl Marx's daughter, who was well aware of the case and sought her out.

Before turning thirteen, Elsa had studied dance with Isadora and Raymond Duncan, taught dance to younger children in her neighborhood, and published a magazine to which she was the sole contributor. Later, she posed for the sculptor Jacob Epstein, who was to born to Polish refugees on New York's Lower East Side. After he received money for his first commission, he moved to Paris, where he received his second commission, which was to design Oscar Wilde's tomb for the Père Lachaise cemetery. When the tombstone was unveiled, the French declared it obscene and covered it with a cloth, doubly interring Mr. Wilde. Today, a glass barrier surrounds the tomb because so many people have drawn hearts and messages on it.

After posing for Epstein, Lanchester founded an after-theater nightclub, the Cave of Harmony, frequented by John Maynard Keynes, Evelyn Waugh, Tallulah Bankhead, and Aleister Crowley, who probably never sat at the same table, but should have. According to Lanchester, in her autobiography, *Elsa Lanchester Herself* (1983), Crowley rode a bicycle to the club and "his head was shaved and he wore a yellow kilt." She did not describe what Bankhead wore.

In *Lifeboat* (1944), directed by Alfred Hitchcock, Bankhead, who described herself as "pure as the driven slush," had to climb a ladder every morning to reach the water tank where the movie was being filmed, and where the rest of the cast was waiting for her to show up. When Bankhead arrived on the set a large crowd always quickly gathered around the water tank to watch her slowly ascend the ladder. To make her arrival and ascent memorable but without unnecessary fanfare, Bankhead thought it would be best to be discreet and simply wear no underwear. When a disconcerted witness brought Bankhead's personal peep show to Hitchcock's attention, he replied: "I don't know if this is a matter for the costume department, makeup, or hair dressing." But this all took place in Lanchester and Bankhead's future, which we have not yet reached.

In 1936, a year after being blown to smithereens by her ungainly monster husband, Lanchester returned to life to play Peter Pan in J. M. Barrie's play, *Peter Pan; or, The Boy Who Wouldn't Grow Up*, which was being performed to great applause at the London Palladium. Lanchester's real husband, Charles Laughton, played Captain Hook, who Barrie described as being "never more sinister than when he was being polite, which is probably the truest test of breeding." Lanchester and Laughton would go on to star together in twelve films, as well as act in Bertolt Brecht's play, *Galileo*, which was staged in Los Angeles in 1947, directed by Joseph Losey, who was born in La Crosse, Wisconsin, where he and Nicholas Ray were classmates at La Crosse Central High School.

While Lanchester and Laughton were parrying in *Peter Pan*, across the English Channel and beyond France, Belgium, and Netherlands, which hugged the coast, the Olympics were being held in Berlin, Germany, as they are now being held in Beijing, China, where you cannot buy Peking duck or publish poems critical of the government.

Years later, the black athlete Jesse Owens, who won four gold medals in Berlin, told a news reporter the greatest ovations he received in his lifetime were in that city, three years after Hitler and the Nazi Party had come to power, and not in America during the presidency of Franklin Delano Roosevelt. Although it is a myth that has been repeated many times because it is easier to believe than the truth, neither Hitler nor the Germans snubbed Owens. It was Roosevelt and America. When Owens returned to America he received no congratulations from President Roosevelt. There were seventeen Black American athletes at the 1936 Olympics. They won fourteen of the fifty-six medals awarded to the American athletes. None of them were invited to the White House.

I was reminded of *The Bride of Frankenstein*, the 1936 Olympics, Hollywood characters, poetry, and marriage, when I read this observation in John Houseman's review of her autobiography: "Miss Lanchester's memoirs are filled with [. . .] frank, vivid and sometimes tasteless impressions of friends and enemies [. . .]." Houseman's remark followed Lanchester's description of Brecht, who smoked cheap cigars and lived with her and Laughton during the rehearsal of *Galileo*: "passing through Brecht, the smoke came out with the sourest, bitterest smell. [. . .] He hadn't many teeth and his mouth opened in a complete circle so you'd see two little tombstones sticking out of this black hole. A very unpleasant sight."

Thinking of Lanchester's description, I wondered if she and Laughton are interred in or around Los Angeles, in a cemetery that has the word "green" in it, lying side by side in perpetuity, something they seldom did in life.

Constance Dowling's Eyes

The seed of this story was planted in Turin in the early 1990s, after I met the reclusive artist Nicola De Maria, who, in the late 1980s, sent me one of his catalogs, *Parole Cinesi* (1985–86) (trans: Chinese Words) and a letter introducing himself. In the winter of 1988, after further correspondence, I flew to Milan and took a train to Turin, where I met Nicola at the station. That first afternoon we walked along the Po River and he recited the opening lines of "Howl" in English. The zoo was closed because of the cold. That was the beginning of our friendship, and over the next fifteen years we saw each other around a half dozen times, always in Turin.

I think the writer and gallerist Jean Fremon—who I met earlier—must have given Nicola my address. Fremon is a writer and was—in the 1980s— one of the three partners running Galerie Lelong & Co., which represented De Maria. The other partners were the poet and friend of Giacometti and Miró, Jacques Dupin, who I met in a bar in New York in the mid-1980s, and Daniel Lelong, who Jean introduced me to in Paris. He was sitting in his office, behind a large desk, and did not invite me in.

Fremon is described as being an important contributor to the "trans-genre tendency in contemporary French letters." Both he and Dupin were friends of the writer Marcel Cohen, who had written to me in the early 1980s, after receiving a copy of my book, *Broken Off by the Music* (1981), which had been published by Keith and Rosmarie Waldrop under their imprint, Burning Deck. In 1995, the Waldrops published Cohen's *The Peacock Emperor Moth,* short stories translated from the French by Cid Corman. This is how one reader described Cohen's work: "Here's how to write novels in two or three or four sentences. The headmaster of that strange school is Cohen." When I met Cohen, Fremon, and Dupin in Paris in the mid-1980s, they did not know that I had already met or been in contact with the others.

It was this series of orbits, which got me to meet Nicola, who is central to the story, though I don't believe the event I am referring to happened during this first visit. It was during another visit that he took me to a bar (or what Americans call a café) one afternoon. I know this didn't happen when we first met because the weather was warm and there was no snow on the ground.

It may have been on this trip that we drove outside of Turin to walk in the fields where Julius Caesar assembled his legions before crossing the Alps.

The choice was deliberate, as everything was with Nicola. He and the owner knew each other, though not well (it seemed to me). They spoke briefly, and introductions were made. I was presented as "poeta americano."

Nicola and I stood at the bar waiting for the owner to bring us our espressos. When he brought them over, he began speaking to me in passable English, asking if I knew of the poet, Cesare Pavese. As soon as I said, "yes," he pointed to an empty table in a separate room, by a small window and secluded from the other tables. "That is where Pavese and the American actress used to meet in the afternoons." He shook his head. "It all ended badly when she said, no," and said no more. At this, Nicola stiffened and became noticeably agitated. We finished our coffee in silence and left.

The owner never mentioned the actress's name, nor did Nicola tell me later, when we were walking to his studio. I only remember him saying "brutal," a word he used whenever he found something to be violent or ugly. In this case, he never said what exactly was "brutal" about this encounter, as he did when he shook his head and said of Pablo Picasso's and Jackson Pollock's paintings, "too brutal." He also expressed dissatisfaction with the owner, but I cannot remember what it was that so irked him. I think Nicola was offended by the owner's gossipy, concierge-like fascination with Pavese's suicide, but I am not sure. I do know that we never went back to that bar, even after I said that I wanted to talk to the owner again, as I was curious about the "American actress." Nicola's response made it clear that it was not a topic open for discussion. Was De Maria, a devout Catholic, distressed because Pavese had committed suicide and that the owner had glorified it in some way?

De Maria had gotten a degree in medicine, with a specialization in psychiatry, but never practiced it. He was a self-taught artist whose life was changed when he met the artists Mario and Marisa Merz. After graduating, De Maria moved to Turin, where he began drawing and painting. He soon began painting directly on walls. In an interview he described himself as: "one who writes poems with his hands soaked in colors." In *Parole Cinesi*, De Maria made small colorful landscape abstractions, each of which he signed with the name of a Chinese artist. It is why I went to meet him.

I do not remember when I learned that the actress's name was Constance Dowling. I must have looked it up, but I don't remember doing this or when. In July 2014, in emails that I sent to Tom Nozkowski and John Ashbery, I mention Dowling, as I had recently seen her in *Blind Spot* (1947), which also starred Chester Morris and Steve Geray, and was directed by Robert Gordon, at the Museum of Modern Art's film series: *Lady in the Dark: Crime Films from Columbia Pictures, 1932–1957*. This was how the museum described the film:

> Taking a break from Columbia's Boston Blackie series, aging matinee idol Chester Morris stars as a vividly alcoholic author of pulp novels who falls under suspicion when his penny-pinching publisher is murdered by a method described in one of his stories. With a screenplay by Martin Goldsmith, the author of the novel that became Edgar G. Ulmer's *Detour*, this casually sordid, micro-budgeted noir features some inventive staging by the director Robert Gordon, including a one-shot, subjective camera scene strikingly similar to a famous sequence in Ulmer's film, as well as a rare sympathetic performance by the professional femme fatale Constance Dowling, whose romantic rejection of the Italian poet Cesare Pavese contributed to his suicide.

I think the program notes, and the mention of Dowling as "a professional femme fatale," which they never substantiated, was the only reason I went to see the film. According to the listing, I saw *Blind Spot* on July 21, 2014, at 6:45 p.m.

I told myself that the other reason I was going was because of Martin Goldsmith. *Detour* (1945), directed by Edgar G. Ulmer, and starring Tom Neal and Ann Savage, is one of my favorite noir films. In real life, the main actor Tom Neal had what De Maria would call a "brutal" temper and was later convicted of manslaughter. His career ended because of his relationship with the actress Barbara Payton, whose highpoint was starring with James Cagney in *Kiss Tomorrow Goodbye* (1950), and making 5,000 a week. That year, Payton met and became engaged to the actor Franchot Tone, while starting an affair with Tom Neal. Payton was very public about this triangle, which enraged Neal. On September 14, 1951, Neal, who had boxed while in college, physically attacked Tone at Payton's apartment, leaving Tone in an eighteen-hour coma with a smashed cheekbone, broken nose, and concussion. Even after she married Tone, Payton continued her affair with Neal, which led to Tone being granted a divorce in 1952. By 1951, Payton's star was losing its shine, as she starred in the low-budget horror *Bride of the Gorilla*, with Raymond Burr.

Neal's co-star, Ann Savage is hardly a sympathetic character, but her grating voice and acting are memorable, particularly because of lines, such as "Stop makin' noises like a husband."

Described as "The Meanest Woman in Film History" and as an "Unglamorous Psycho Villainess," Savage played forgettable roles in bad films for a decade (1943–1953) and is remembered only for being the hitchhiker, Vera, in *Detour*.

In 1985, Savage talked about her roles during the 1940s to the *Los Angeles Times*:

> They were mindless. The actresses were just scenery. The stories all revolved around the male actors; they really had the choice roles. All the actresses had to do was to look lovely, since the dialogue was ridiculous.

How did Dowling last as long as she did if she only gave unsympathetic performances? Isn't there something memorable about her besides her known effect on Pavese?

On July 31, 2014, Ashbery wrote back:

I never heard of *Blind Spot*, and I must shamefully admit to not having heard of Constance Dowling either, though I of course know her sister, Doris, who was in Italian post-war neo-realist movies, e.g. *Bitter Rice*. We really should compare notes some time.

Later that day, I wrote to John:

Doris is probably the reason Constance went to Italy. She also starred in some Italian neo-realist films. When I used to go to Turin to see a painter friend, we once had coffee in the shop where Pavese and Constance would meet. I just got *Black Angel* starring Dan Duryea, Peter Lorre and June Vincent (Dowling has a bit part), which Andrew Sarris considers one of the "25 most memorable cult films."

I think Sarris's description of *Black Angel* was why I wrote to Tom. Three years later, in an email dated January 17, 2017, I learned that in "March or April 1964," Nozkowski had dropped out of school, partly because he had just finished reading writings by Andrew Sarris that would appear in *The American Cinema: Directors and Directions 1929–1968*, a guide to over 200 film directors and an alphabetical listing of 6000 films, listing their directors and years they were released. When the book came out, Tom used it as a guide to directors and films he had not seen or taken seriously. After driving cross country and visiting friends in San Francisco and Los Angeles, and sharing a cabin with friends in Lowell, Vermont, he "came back to the city mid-Winter. The first order of business was to see Godard's *Contempt* which had just opened to the worst possible reviews and was sure to quickly disappear." Someone as dedicated to film as Tom was must have known about Constance Dowling, but I can find no comment from him about her or Doris in our extensive email correspondence.

I was wrong. Constance, who was Doris's older sister, moved to Rome first, hoping to revive her career. She had played female leads, but was starting to be moved further down the credits list. According to her IMDb biography,

Once she started moving further down the credits list, as she was for the Republic film noir, *The Flame* (1947), which starred studio mogul Herbert J. Yates' wife Vera Ralston [who, I would add, was forty years younger than her husband], she decided to move to Italy and try and maintain her leading lady career there.

Ralston was born in Prague and had achieved modest success as a figure skater. She placed fifteenth in the 1936 European Figure Skating Championships and seventeenth in the 1936 Winter Olympics. According to Ralston, when Adolph Hitler asked her if she would like to "skate for the swastika," she told him that she would "rather skate on it." In Hollywood, because of her limited English skills, she normally played the part of a young immigrant woman. Because of her marriage to Yates, she was able to star in twenty movies, only two of which made money.

Constance's younger sister Doris, who by 1947 had achieved a modest degree of popularity, moved to Rome a short time later. I have seen a photo of Doris Dowling and Cesare Pavese standing together, but not one of Constance and him. Together, the Dowling sisters became the first American actresses to work exclusively in Italian films, which means they were bilingual, unlike Ralston. Her circle of friends included Alberto Moravia, Ernest Hemingway, Jean Paul Sartre, and Robert Capra.

Constance never gained the attention that her sister Doris did, either in America or Italy. In 1946, the year before Constance starred in *Blind Spot*, "Bad Girl," an article by Frank Chapman, appeared on page 48 of the January 20, 1946 issue of *The Post-Standard*, a newspaper serving the metro area of Syracuse, New York:

> If Ray Milland's performance in the movie of Charlotte Jackson's *Lost Weekend* doesn't win him the Academy Award for 1945, then there is, of course, no hope for Hollywood. The Irish-born Monsoor Milland makes this teeth-rattling story of a drunk one of the tours de force of all time; he wraps up the picture and carries it home with him in the inside jacket pocket with the fifth of bourbon. Acting like that is knitted in the laps of the gods.

Against this razzle-dazzle witchery, the neat but not gaudy efforts of players like Jane Wyman and Phil Terry are swallowed and forgotten—hopelessly swamped by the floodtide of emotion that Milland turns loose. But for a few memorable scenes—scenes that are tender and, Lord preserve us, poignant— Mr. Milland has some big league company. This is a dark-haired, high-cheekboned, sexotic piece of baggage named Doris Dowling—playing in the first movie she ever made in her life.

Chapman was right, of course, Milland won the Academy Award and Cannes Film Festival Award for his portrayal of an alcoholic writer in *Lost Weekend*. Later, in his profile of Doris, Chapman quotes her:

> The public may like the ingenues, but they remember the witches. I want to do a couple of those until I get my feet firmly on the ladder. In a way, I'm glad that Ray did such a terrific job in the first movie I made, because it sort of buries me and lets me climb slowly. If I were good enough to ring the bell the first time out and make the critics click their heels, I'd be terrified—terrified that I couldn't live up to the inevitable buildup. That's happened not too long ago, you know.

Constance Dowling never got this kind of write-up. She got on the ladder as a second-liner in B films, because she was a "Goldwyn Girl," who was briefly favored by Samuel Goldwyn, before he turned his attention to Virgina Mayo. She was never able to climb higher or star in a breakthrough film. She never got to write her own ticket, as they say.

Constance previously had second billing with Chester Morris in *Boston Blackie and the Law* (1946), which was likely why they were paired again in *Blind Spot*. There is no on-screen magic between them, though this did not prevent Carole Lombard and Fred MacMurray from appearing in four films together at Paramount between 1935 and '37. According to Steve Vineberg, Distinguished Professor of the Arts and Humanities at the College of the Holy Cross in Worcester, Massachusetts, "It's easy to fall in love with [Lombard]; everything about her is endearing, including her nuttiness." No one ever described Dowling as endearing. In fact, there are almost no descriptions of her on-screen personality, her acting. It is almost as if she was not in the movies she was in.

After his relationship with Dowling ended, Pavese wrote in his diary:

> One does not kill oneself for love of a woman, but because love—any love—reveals us in our nakedness, our misery, our vulnerability, our nothingness.

In an essay that appeared in the *American Poetry Review* (September/October, 1997), Alan Williamson wrote:

> At first, Constance Dowling seemed the inconceivable remedy to this whole history of failure. Partly, it was simply because she was American. Pavese had long had a romance with what seemed to him the pragmatic yet innocent freshness in American culture; he had translated not only *Moby Dick* but many populist works of the twenties and thirties—Steinbeck, Sherwood Anderson, even Sinclair Lewis. At first he felt rejuvenated with Constance, restored to a self-confidence he did not know he possessed: "It was a terrible step, yet I took it. Her incredible sweetness, her 'Darlings,' her smile, her long-repeated pleasure at being with me. Nights at Cervinia, nights at Turin. She is a child, an unspoiled child. Yet she is herself—terrifying. From the bottom of my heart, I did not deserve so much." (16th March, 1950).

Not all went smoothly. One night, in Milan, Pavese told his biographer, David Lajolo:

> She fled at night from my bed at the hotel in Rome and she went to bed with another, with that actor you know. Like the other woman, even worse. Do you remember the one from Turin? She is the one who ended it between me and women.

Shortly after Constance turned down Pavese's marriage proposal and flew back to America, He wrote a poem in his diary that begins with a line (literally translated):

"Death Will Come and Will Have Your Eyes."

It will be the title of his final book of poetry, causing a scandal because two months after they separated, Pavese checked into a hotel in Turin and took a fatal overdose of sleeping pills.

The poem links love and morbidity.

Later on in the poem, Pavese writes,

> It will be like ending a vice,
> like seeing a dead face
> emerge from the mirror,
> like hearing closed lips speak.

Is this what it is like to sit in a dark auditorium and watch "lovely, exotic looking, hazel-eyed blonde Constance Dowling" appear on screen? She is never on screen long enough; the camera does not stare at her, even if there are those in the audience who want to.

The last film Dowling was in was the cult sci-fi flick, *Gog* (1954), about two robots, Gog and Magog in a secret underground laboratory in New Mexico, which are being controlled by an enemy robot plane. Dowling's role was to be a love interest and to scream. She was in her midthirties.

The independently made film was produced by Ivan Tors, who was interested in nonviolent science fiction movies and stories starring animals. His animal films include *Flipper* (1963), *Flipper's New Adventure* (1964), *Zebra in the Kitchen* (1965), but there is disagreement over wheather he or his company produced *Clarence the Cross-Eyed Lion* (1965).

Tors and Dowling were married from 1955 to 1969, when she died of a heart attack at the age of forty-nine. They had four children, three of whom were in the film, *Escape from Angola* (1976). During the 1960s, she worked as a guide at the Dolphin Laboratory in St. Thomas, in the US Virgin Islands. She is buried at Holy Cross Cemetery, Culver City, California.

Doris Dowling's career took a different turn. She appeared in over sixty films, often typecast as wife, mother, old maid, busybody, aristocrat, gold digger, con artist, eccentric, femme fatale, landlady, neighbor, curmudgeon, reporter, secretary, nurse, politician, exotic, indigenous person, foreigner, doctor, clergywoman, retail clerk, businesswoman, and, in her later years, matriarch. She died in 2004, more than thirty years after Constance, and is also interred at Holy Cross Cemetery.

A few days ago, I began this piece after reading Doug Lang's sonnet, "Unheard Melodies Endure," which contains the line: "Cesare Pavese loved Constance Dowling."

It was like reading graffiti on a wall somewhere, a testament that someone had left behind.

Acknowledgments

I would like to thank the following magazines and editors for giving my work a place to exist physically and digitally:

Agni (Jennifer Kwon Dobbs), *Big Other* (John Madera), *Brooklyn Rail* (Anselm Berrigan), *Conjunctions* (Brad Morrow) *Evergreen Review* (Jee Leong Koh), *Itinerant* (Bianca Stone), *LiVE Mag!* (Jeff Wright), *Marsh Hawk Review* (Thomas Fink), *Trilobite* (Paul Vogel)

I am grateful to the following editors for selecting my work:

Arthur Sze for selecting "Charles Baudelaire and I Meet at the Oval Garden" to be recorded for *Poem-a-Day*.

Elaine Equi, editor of *The Best American Poetry 2023* (Scribner), for selecting "Song for Mie Yim."

Many thanks go to the following individuals for supporting my work:

Ian Heames for publishing an earlier version of "Elsa and Charles with Cameo by Tallulah" in the Earthbound Poetry Series (London, UK, 2022)

Pia Fries for inviting me to write a series of poems, "Too Far to Write Down," in response to her work, *tausend: einerlei* (Keinbaum Artists' Books, 2023), and to Stefan Weidle for translating the poems into German.

I want to thank the following individuals for reading and responding to earlier versions of the works included in the book you are holding, and for helping give this book the shape it has taken:

Anselm Berrigan, Albert Mobilio, Billie Chernicoff, and Joseph Donahue

About the Author

John Yau is the author of many books, including, most recently, a selection of essays, *Please Wait by the Coatroom: Reconsidering Race and Identity in American Art* (Black Sparrow, 2023), a monograph, *Joe Brainard: the Art of the Personal* (Rizzoli Electa, 2022), and a volume of poetry, *Genghis Chan on Drums* (Omnidawn, 2021). He received the 2018 Jackson Poetry Prize, a Rabkin Award for his art criticism in 2021, and the Culture-Warren Award for poetry from the Hunan Academy of Poetry in 2022. He lives and works in New York.

Tell It Slant

by John Yau

Cover art by Eve Ascheim, "Steel and Soaking" (2013), 18 x 14 inches, oil and graphite on canvas on panel. By permission of the artist.

Cover design and interior design by Shanna Compton

Cover typefaces: Museo Sans and Calluna Sans
Interior typefaces: Adobe Garamond Pro and Museo Sans

Printed in the United States
by Books International, Dulles, Virginia

Publication of this book was made possible in part by gifts from Katherine & John Gravendyk in honor of Hillary Gravendyk, Francesca Bell, Mary Mackey, and The New Place Fund

Omnidawn Publishing   Oakland, California

Staff and Volunteers, Fall 2023

Rusty Morrison senior editor & co-publisher
Laura Joakimson, executive director and co-publisher
Rob Hendricks, poetry & fiction editor, & post-pub marketing
Jason Bayani, poetry editor
Anthony Cody, poetry editor
Liza Flum, poetry editor
Kimberly Reyes, poetry editor
Sharon Zetter, poetry editor & book designer
Jeffrey Kingman, copy editor
Jennifer Metsker, marketing assistant
Sophia Carr, marketing assistant
Katie Tomzynski, marketing assistant